A Poetry Encyclopedia of Dreams

Jakob Brønnum

Copyright© 2025 Jakob Brønnum
ISBN: 978-93-6354-534-2

First Edition: 2025
Rs. 200/-

Cyberwit.net
HIG 45 Kaushambi Kunj, Kalindipuram
Allahabad - 211011 (U.P.) India
http://www.cyberwit.net
Tel: +(91) 9415091004
E-mail: info@cyberwit.net

No part of this book may be reproduced or transmitted in any form or by any means, electronic, mechanical, photocopying, or otherwise, without the express written consent of Jakob Brønnum.

Printed at Repro India Limited.

Preface

This is a handbook of dream interpretation in the form of poems.

Handbooks interpreting dreams in detail abound and have done for centuries. The entries mirror the times in which the book was written, resulting in entries like dreams about abbeys and abbesses, virgins, princes and frogs.

Many modern attempts to interpret dreams mimic Freud and especially Jungian symbolism. The latter tends to be looking for images to be interpreted according to proposed archetypes.

Surprisingly enough, the magisterial volume Dreaming (2005) in the popular series A Very Short Introduction by Oxford University Press maintain that dreams have no meaning in the classic sense, but speculates whether dream imagery is a product of a form of psychosis in the mind during sleep when consciousness is on hold.

Where does this leave this book, A Poetry Encyclopedia of Dreams? Poetic language is devoid of intent in the realm of meaning. Still, meaning arises when the dream image is met by poetry.

And the poetry? Some of it is grotesque, some banal, some of it very dark, some of it unreasonably bright and light of heart. Just like dreams. Some of the wording is analytic, nerdy, and overexplanatory. Just like encyclopedias.

The collection is a companion volume to my book Dreamscape Journeys (Cyberwit, 2025). Thanks are due to Kathrina Martinsen for solid help with the manuscript.

JB, Jan. 2025

Contents

The Letter A

Whoever sees an A in dreams
upside down
may interpret it as the sacred bull roaming
the vast plains of Asia
long before the time of Zarathustra

Whoever sees an A in dreams
upside down
is in trouble. You need to wake up
having done things right

or face the consequence. You must
bend your mind
and make known to eternity: This is not The Bull of Heaven

as the sages had it, this is merely the letter A
turned upside down

(I didn't do it. You didn't do it? Who did it then? It just happened
to be that way. Who cares? I care. Why do you care?)

Adventure

According to The Official Dream Register
there are currently too few dreams concerning *adventure*
to conclude anything statistically significant

This could point to the fact
that adventure might not exist
for the time being
or that adventure has been absolved
by consumer activities
and covered in blurred photographs

A good few dreams, however, are concerned
with urban dystopia and the panic attack preceding

a recurrent dream
everybody experiences
at least once a month
is the parallel dream
about being left alone
on the dance floor

like people turning away from you
when you need them most

The Andes

In dreams, sometimes we all climb
to the heights of Machu Picchu

hoping to let the spirit
carry us to where the air loses its colors

hoping to climb into
the mouth of Pablo Neruda

There is always a chance he is standing
on a corner somewhere

smoking a cigarette
wearing a blue raincoat

His black shoes from the fifties
casually resting upon a rock

that rolled down here in ancient times
broken off from a cliff in heaven

Albatross

Overhead the albatross
Hangs motionless upon the air
And deep beneath the rolling waves
In labyrinths of coral caves
The echo of a distant time
(Pink Floyd)

Everybody has dreamt about being an albatross
soaring over the deep blue sea
and the deep black sea and the white sea

some dreams never really end
some dreamers feel they are doomed to soar
some dreamers begin to freeze

Everybody has dreamt about soaring
what they thought to be the ocean
and discovered it was a parking lot

Ape

Nobody ever dreamt they were an ape
though we all learned that in school. Sometimes

we climb trees without
knowing of apes. We only know of ourselves

and maybe the breath we share
with every living being

Some may dream of very apt
hands gripping

trunks of varying thickness
coarse surfaces, as well as looking down from

infinite height

Ariadne

The dreamer says:
Even if I find the thread
I know I shall never see her

This is the point: She was
there before me

and I must ponder over this "before."
What is before? What is before me?

Is it somewhere in time?
Or is it sometime in space? I am the dreamer, I must
locate, find, pick up and weave threads myself

this is the point of the dream
and the point of reality:

Ariadne is where
dream meets reality

Beach, leaving for the (The Stress Dream)

The dream goes like this: All the things we must remember
all the things, all the things
and all the things we know we won't remember
and all that we forgot on purpose

all the running around the house
all of a sudden completely full
of stairs, stairs, stairs

all the trying to find the exact specimen of the selected supplies
all the mess, all the searching in exploding breath
all the things we bring to the beach
finally chosen through deliberation and the rolling of dice,
and the law of inertia, and the second law of thermodynamics

and all the time the motor, the impatient sound
of the car out in the runway
the motor transposing the impatient sun and the hot sand

Then tell me this: Why is it I can never locate any
sunglasses whatsoever
when the world really needs them

Blindfolded

History does know of dreams about being blindfolded
probably everybody has had a go at it, maybe once as a child

Dreaming about being blindfolded could be one of those occurrences
you always hear about from somebody else

who heard about from somebody
who talked to one

who dreamt about being blindfolded
but they just couldn't remember who it was

You do not remember the dream yourself, do you?
I have my doubts: Dreaming is being blindfolded itself

My father told me again and again.
I never believed him. I still miss him.

Burnt Beyond Recognition

Sometimes the dream stumbles over somebody
(literally: some body). The reason you do not recognize this bodily

reminiscence is obvious
and often accompanied by a certain smell

It might be unpleasant but it's
the reality of dreaming

As long as you do not dream
about yourself in this capacity the way is clear:

You shall have a life. And if anybody tells you to get a life
you might state the obvious fact: I have a life. At least

chances are you'll get one. Some dreams
bring other forms of smelly notions

Some dreams carry the smell of incense, some
are laden with memorabilia

Blood

The old ones before us were very scared of blood
in dreams. Dripping blood

was thought to mean somebody was about to die
in unnameable sin

blood-stained garments were thought to symbolize
enemies coming from afar or threats lurking within

Now everything is biology.
There is no "my blood" and "your blood." Dreaming about blood means

dreaming about sameness, likeness and breath, dreaming
about skin so very close to you. Precious skin

or just broken glass

Cicada

The dreamer says: Last night the cicada
sang in my dream

and I experienced the utmost bliss, the apotheosis.
This is true. Because when the cicada sings
there is no connection to time or space

there is no individuality
during the dream the song forms a face woven in clouds

and you know instantly what the dream
will tell you: It is sound and yet no sound

because it is pure heartbeat. It is the origin
of dream revealing itself to the dreamer.

The dreamer says: Last night the cicada sang
in my dream

Coconut Anxiety

Dreaming about coconuts is prohibited
in certain parts of the Pacific

and on Key West
(dreams about coconut flakes do not count)

If you hear a noise like something falling
on a hard surface

and you see a palm tree
in the vicinity of your dream

don't laugh
lest you shall be haunted

by the gho-ghost
for the rest of your anxiety

Code, Breaking the

There are dreams that mean something specific by way
of communicating with your memory

by way of being logged on to that inner tv-screen
you do not turn off and on yourself

There are dreams that mean something
but do not have the slightest intention of letting you know what

The motor in your mind
will subconsciously work on breaking the code
all during the day

not knowing if such a code
exists at all. The dream itself is the code. It might break

Coffee

If you wake up right after having received
the most delicious cup of coffee
as if interrupted right before entering into
the enjoyment itself, this will be the moment of truth
the way dreams always contain one or more paths
to knowledge. One should refrain from expressing anger

over the said missed enjoyment
towards the one who woke you up with inferior or no coffee

The meaning of this dream is that you have
a very good day in store for you
making you understand and acknowledge
that you also have the power to completely ruin it

Cycles

The dreamer exclaims: I dreamt about a cycle of ballets
with people in them nobody recognizes

The dreamer says: I dreamt about the cycle of the moon
winding its way around a planet of hearts

the hearts falling out of people's hands
as they were trying to cling on to them

The dreamer: I dreamt of a cycle of walking
in and out of empty houses

suddenly reminded of cycles of
flowers and rhymes, long forgotten

There were cycles, cycles of seasons and of love
cycles of blood, cycles of good and evil

Never returning to the starting point
before the dream was over. No tears. Just energy

and yearning

Disgust, Expressions of

In this dream, if you happen to be floating on a layer
of exquisite summer clouds
not cold at all, nothing to worry about
why would there be expressions of disgust

This is the strange thing about it all: You float
in the most beautiful setting ever thought out
by angels and/or architects and you've just seen
the most beautiful butterfly that ever laid its

wings to rest on the wind

and you find it disgusting. The beauty disgusts you
and you don't know why, but you know it's true
and then there is the girl with the brown hair
and her unforgettable eyes (her eyes: un•for•get•ta•ble)

who disappeared in the long grass over the hill
when you lived there and everything still
was devoid of worries and now you want to hurt something
or someone, even and/or most probably yourself

Diving

Dreams of swimming underwater share a different nature
from dreams of falling
and dreams of mountain climbing

and they share a different nature
from dreams about sailing under the summer skies
and dreams about crossing the Atlantic
in a balloon
and from dreams about being lost
in a mineshaft left unused since the century before last

Dreams about diving
is about being almighty and yet unborn
they are about being the subject
of gravitational forces and possessing
the essence of life
they are about a love visionary

and about knowing how much an embrace
will carry you

upwards, upwards

Drawing (The Panic Dream)

The dreamer explains:
I used to draw little sketches

everybody used to draw
little sketches

everybody dropped
their pencil sometimes

everybody dreams about
panicking because they find no paper

and there is a world at war
and if they don't find a sheet of paper

they will not remember what they saw
and so wanted to sketch

in due course to achieve
peace in our time

Dragonfly

Often it is said that dragonflies symbolize change
because they achieve a new form
through every phase of life

Other sources mention the dragonfly
as a symbol of power
since it moves effortlessly in all directions

It is otherwise universally recognized that the dragonfly
is the proponent of a beauty
unfathomable by human emotionality

Dreaming you are a dragonfly is a dream
about autumn nearing
and we all know what that means for a dragonfly

But we don't know for sure what it means
for you and me

Eagle

This dream is naked instinct,
prophetic promise
from the well of eternal dream weaving

whosoever see the eagle soaring
may, shall, and will consider
themselves blessed

You may dream about climbing
the mountain aiming
for the eagle's precious eggs

or you may be trapped
in that eternal dream
about being prisoner in the eagle's nest

Easter Island

To be left on Easter Island in a dream
is a faith worse than eternal fasting

praying to become a head tumbled in grass
to survive, breathing on the edge of The Pacific

with no one left to talk with
and with no smoke ever rising on the horizon

Elimination During Dreams

Any elimination that has come over you
could be reset during breakfast, unless (Unless what?)

Any elimination you have caused
trusting no one has noticed it yet

though your hands are still wet and cold
could be reset, unless (Unless what?)

Any elimination that has come upon you
and caused you to roam around cityscapes

breathlessly conquering mountainous areas
with holes in your soul and a body of fragments

Any elimination of property, ecosystems
oceans, used dreams, silly wars

full of dust and debris and blood and sadness
any elimination of values that you held

could be reset during a solid breakfast, unless
Unless, unless, unless it can't

Egg

The witness says: I always dreamt
I would dream about the egg

about what came first: The dream
about the egg or the egg

or the dream about sleeping inside the egg
to see whether light in there was as beautifully

orange and yellow
as I thought

so beautifully pearly
that you would never have to dream again

or whether the dream
simply had life of its own

wanting to get rid of you by making you forget
you are in fact a mammalian beast

Elvis

From The Cosmic Encyclopedia:
Whoever dreams of Elvis

sees him stepping out
dressed in white, sequins glittering

Elvis' voice is always present somewhere
The Elvis Dream is the gift of being able to hear his voice

as alive as you or me
it is the blessing of knowing

deep within your sequin-glittering soul
that he never left the building at all

Emojis

Sometimes we need to dream about emojis

Sometimes we have dreams
about how we can find only sad emojis
on the phone

You might feel it's life itself intervening
changing the emojis on your phone

This could very well be the case

We cannot decide what kind of dreams we have
but we do have a certain influence over their stories

Enemy/enemies

This is pure illusion. Enemies don't exist
in dreams. They are versions
of yourself you do not like (understandably)

How do enemies disappear? How to win over your own best enemy?
How to win the war inside yourself?

The dream will end soon enough
but you can always go back to its message
since you have it present in your body all day long

Ex

The dream about being doomed to live
with your ex, with the only way out
to be doomed to live with your ex before that
What on earth is this dream about?

This dream is about going somewhere else
this dream is about going places you
never imagined, like back to basics
but not the basics you thought you knew

this dream is about the need to step outside
to surpass time as you know it
to break out of the holster of identity

Falcon

Dreams in which the falcon occur
are very important. Even the dream says
this: You must listen carefully

and you must be alert, and you must be ready to read any sign
and you must be ready to make decisions and be ready to follow

and to be prepared
to dig up any old memories
that may contain hints

Do you see the people out there in the distance
ready to send out the falcon? They are called falconers

you must listen to them too, very carefully
you must make time go as slow as possible, they know the wind

Fields

The sources assert: There is no end to these fields
there is no end to the rolling
and to the goddess guarding wheat
there is no end to the scent of chaff and dust

there are things you cannot leave,
there are things you wait for
by destiny and motivation

among these are rain, people's faces, new mornings
suddenly turning up
from beyond the rising hills

from the rolling dream that I am caught in
until the wind sets me free

Forgetting Your Name

These are the dreams we won't readily talk about
since we do not know what the name means and/or
if it contains part the of the soul
that produces itself as a physical entity
upon hearing the name pronounced
or even whispered
or if it is just a holster your parents put you in
to make you fit their rendition of you in the beginning

These are dreams about either losing the knowledge
of who you are or realizing that you never fully attained it

Forgetting where you Live

This belongs to a certain group of dreams
concerning the unfortunate consequences of Neoliberalism

the assets of your old age pension
the plants you forget to water

the hopes you had in youth
now unhappily forgotten and erased

from the screens of your conscious mind,
the intensity of your honesty on a daily basis

and the amount of poison stored in your vocabulary

Friends

In the dream about friends
either you have friends
or you have none

either your friends are honest
and you are not
or your friends have left you
because you are who you are and/or
because you want to change

In the dream about friends either you keep being late
for the gathering and every time you arrive
the pizza is eaten, or they have saved a piece for you

but you have no money
and dare not ask

and/or you discover that's what friends are for
but you don't like them

Gift, receiving a

Receiving a gift in dreams
is a test to inform you

whether your secret heart talks about
giving or deserving

if you picture your wealth
or the other person's joy

Whether you open it right away
or wait till afterwards

till they are gone
to make sure to conceal

any unwanted sentiments.
It is how you receive it

how your hands move
how your fingers are positioned

in the event

Giraffe

Legends says that if ever you dream
about the giraffe you shall never die

it will show you how to see
so that you never again have to just look

you will attain patience with the flaws
in the soul that you carry around
like a ton of lead

There will be elevation and the love of foliage

the dream will show you cosmos
above the trees
where time and eternity
finally connected in an everlasting kiss

Glass

Glass in dreams is a sign of walls and mountains
hindering you. The truth is right
in front of you
but you cannot achieve it

Glass in dreams is a symbol of things
you know well you ought to
take care of
because it is obvious
but you don't do it, and you don't know why

Glass in dreams is prophetic
the way you never know if it's true
until it has happened

Glass in dreams is like truth and blood
you know it's there
but you don't see it, you simply don't

Hand

Most dreamers regard the appearance
of a hand a priceless gift

(most forget the first hand they ever met was their mother's)

Most dreamers are disappointed
and have a hard time

coping with the fact that a hand in a dream
is only a shadow
reminiscent only by chance

Hawk

The problem with the concept of hawk in your dreams
is that a lot of it is pure hawkishness
and most of the rest is the fear of having something
diving down upon you and your scalp from murky skies
as well as the fear of having to run faster than you can
and being overcome by your own breath exploding
and the anxiety of having mice mingling at your feet

knowing that the hawk is a symbol of instincts
you do not possess and have no way of decoding

Hanged man

Some symbols carry the irony themselves:
Look at the hanged man. No matter which way you see it,

you know. You know all there is to know,
and you know nothing. You know how a smile

is never for free. Either you pay
or the other pays

You know the sense of loss comes
not without a sense of gain. And vice versa. You just know.
That's what the dreams say. The dream knows

House

There is never a straightforward house in dreams
either it is endlessly labyrinthine
or a dump, full of things you forgot you bought

or a tower with broken walls
and a grey storm
blowing under your t-shirt
from beneath (and it's really annoying)

and there is someone at the door
but you still can't find the door

Ice

You look at the Arctic Ocean from above

You wake up in the ice, but you are still dreaming

You never saw such blue in your whole life

You never felt so cold and still laughing

You never knew you were at one with your body

You never knew your body was an ocean

Ice cream, melting

Loud screams in your head. Youth, slowly
but surely waning. Panic attack alert

Doomed to stand naked
with all your friends around (because

your trousers are stained and will be sent off to dry
cleaning). The poles in your brain disappearing,

just melting away. Obesity. Nature in pain

Inheritance

Very few dreams are about inheritance
and the ones that are tend to be rather slimy

There is in dreams a lack of rich uncles hitherto unknown
there is a distinct lack of extra money

but you do tend to inherit problems, bad breath, unplanned
events, chaotic weather and flat tires on buses
that were late in the first place

You do tend to inherit moral nausea
bodily pain
and endless yearning

Jesus, Walking on the Water

Seeing Jesus walk on the water, you say:
Wtf! Looking down
you'll feel your feet are cold

and you see
that you yourself are
walking on water

and you know
that if you think anything about it -
anything whatsoever

ever so slightly
pretending this is not normal

you will begin to sink

Job

These recurrent dreams of Job
scraping the scab
with his favorite pot shard
and the shadows of three people
sliding over his head

compelling him to ask these recurrent
questions: Are they friends
are the foes, are they angry, do they pity him, poor Job

while he raises his fist at heaven like Beethoven
either cursing his maker
or the drought

while his throat dries up
while his mind dries up and knows no more words
while he tries to understand the world

and the stupid media, Suddenly
the wind begins to blow
dust upon my face and in my eyes

Oh Lord! Please don't take Job away
he is our witness; he is a man of clay while we
have become men of plastic. Oh Lord,

please let me wake up

Judge, Appearing Before the

Dreaming about judgement is bad
since you never know what you have done

most dreams are immoral
you don't even feel any wrongdoing

dreams try to persuade you to just let go
and then show you that you can't even move

That's how it is to appear before the judge:
You have to let go, but you can't move

Kafka

Dreaming about Kafka spells trouble
you are prone to longing seriously for the morning

but one thing you can be sure of
is that when you reach the morning
it is already gone. If you ask somebody where it is

they will say they've not seen it
they will ask you to try and come back another day

Keyhole

No statistics, no rational thought
will tell us whether there are more keyholes
than keys in this world
solving this issue
is a matter of mansplaining

some argue that there are as many keys
as people carry with them
and that any key whose whereabouts
are unknown does not count

others maintain that there are
many unknown keyholes in this world
and that this fact constitutes an endless amount

Usually, when in a dream you have a key
in your freezing hand
you are on the lookout for a keyhole
when you've finally found it
it carries with it the recognition of the fact

that there is a spider watching you
from the inside

Keys, Finding Your

When I find my keys
I never knew I'd lost them

this means of course
new insight

any dream interpreter
knows that. What nobody knows

is where the lock is
it could be a door, it could be a chest

it could be a heart
But only you can search out the lock

the dream never helps you there
It leaves you with endless tunnels,

labyrinths, pathways
walls and no door in sight

for miles on end
just keys in your hand

Keys, Dropping Them Accidentally in the Sewer

Who knows what the keys will experience
on their way to the ocean, below the pavement
out of sight of man but not of beast

being symbolic keys
to your house

which is either your heart
or your bad conscience

Did you actually drop them on purpose,
just a little bit?

Kiss

Dreamy kissing is everybody's secret
the problem is not the secret
but the fact that there is always
a condition attached

Who wants to kiss
conditionally? Who wants
to carry secrets around
about things that never happened?

Who wants to dream
about kissing when there are no kisses, just

plain air and blurred mirrors

Language, Unintelligible

aka: blab, chatter, clack, gabble,
gibber, gibberish, dreamerish

A desert often appears here
and an elephant

wakeupperish, maunder, palaver,
piffle, prate, prattle, tattle, tittle-tattle

here the little animals are turning out
to be hungry and somewhat ratsy

twaddle, twaddle, twaddle, twaddle, twaddle

There is often a blushing face at this point
before it goes into mere

yammer, yammer

Laughing

Other people laughing in dreams is a tricky business
since there is truly
no way
to assess what they are laughing at
and since it's your dream
the most obvious possibility is that they are laughing at you
though the dream offers no possibilities
of finding out what
you did
or did not do
to make them laugh

Laughing in dreams is a risky business
(no matter whether you laugh because they laugh or because it is funny)
since if you laugh it might be an indication of an incoming fall

Lion

Dreaming about a lion
is a very honorable thing

expect knights in armor
expect labyrinths

expect very cold, dark, and prolonged nights
expect really bad drinking water

expect a reasonable measure of drums, spears,
tattoos, expect no damsels

expect the smell of blood
expect thirst

Love

In the beginning it looks like a snake
but it turns out to be smoke

slowly winding its way towards heaven
through the body of its soulmate, the air

This is no game, the voice says
and yet you sit there

at the round table
moving colored pieces on the board

in the background there is music and laughter
there is clinking of bottles.

This is no game, the voice says
but you're bound to play it anyway

Magician

Many dreams progress as a search for a magician
everybody knows everything can happen
in dreams so you might as well search for a magician

nobody has ever seen a magician IRL
but everybody wants to see one (and secretly,
be one). When he/she/they finally come/s

this demands a kind of attention you simply can't muster
in a dream, it must be something you had with you
when you left home this morning

The magician will take all known concepts of reality
away from the dream and, since you well know
they are there anyway, yet only hidden,

the dream progresses as a search for reality.
When you turn around like Orpheus
you see the pale face of the magician miming:

There's magic. That's magic for you

The Market Reports

Following the market reports in a dream
can be a demanding venture
the goal is to make the numbers
come to a standstill
but they won't. Numbers
move, and keep moving. They are numbers

The whole dream is slipping away through your fingers
but all of a sudden there is the smell of cigar

there is a vague sense
of dangling crystal from the chandelier
that appeared over your head
just now. Still in the background

numbers moving, promenading
across the screen. There is a voice, a man's voice
like a prelate chanting

The whole dream is slipping away through your fingers

Morning Dew

Walk me out in the morning dew, my honey
Walk me out in the morning dew today
I'll walk you out in the morning dew, my honey
I guess it doesn't really matter anyway
(Bonnie Dobson)

Walking out in the morning dew
listening in vain for the birds
trying to catch the wind
with your lips
but there is none. Wondering
what the sun is doing
since the dew never vaporizes. No foliage moving

you begin to wonder
if the trees are made of glass

you begin to wonder if the air
is made of ice

Mushroom

The Dream seer declares: I've seen people stuck in
a dream where they
thought they were mushrooms
many of whom were worried it could be
an alien species

they didn't know where they would pop up the next time
fearing it could be anywhere

yearning for oxygen, yearning for deserts
yearning to be assigned a face
so they could smile

at the other mushrooms

standing in a forest of mushrooms
under a very low ceiling of rainforest magic

at the same time dying for a taste of salt

Naked in a Dream

Being naked in a dream is a good omen
it means that you still have a lot of shame to get rid of

It means that you still possess the ability to freeze
It means that you've finally understood Mahler's 9th

it means that you are not afraid anymore
of anybody but yourself. Philosophically, however
one still wants to know a few things:

How many feel naked even when they are dressed
how many feel ashamed of their own body and envious of others
how many forget they are naked and discover it in the street

Nuclear Winter

Being left in a nuclear winter
discovering it is not even cold
knowing all too well this is a dream

getting an anxiety attack
at the thought of what is going to happen to you
when you awake

trying to button the coat
around you
you don't even have

staring at your hands grappling with empty space

Ocean

It is good to have an ocean in your dream
the ocean is that which will not be misunderstood

sometimes, when you talk about
designing new gods
you always know the ocean is listening

Same goes for talking about money, too

Octopus (The Therapist Dream)

The octopus dream is a question mark
that sometimes gets entangled
in other question marks
each looking like the arms of the wretched creature itself

as if the mystery of the octopus
comes from its ability
to tangle up eight question marks
at a time, more than any therapist ever managed

The octopus dream raises the essential question:

Did you get caught in these question mark-like arms
or did you just need somebody to hold you at the time

Palm

Stretching out your hand in a dream
bears the hope we need now
reading your palm quenches the hope

unless you look further
into the heart
where the dream is weaving

it's funny stories
and fake news about
your hopes, wishes and dreams

A lot of people dreaming about
stretching out their hand
wakes up in shock with the palm

awfully sweaty

Phone (with the Cord Stuck in the Wall)

In the dream with the phone with the cord stuck in the wall
you are very old. The phone is not stuck
at all. You have to follow
the cord towards the wall

to pull it out so you can go around
talking on the phone
with your friends
because they all wait for you to call
or maybe you should just call them to see
if they were waiting

you realize you are on a bridge
between two mountains

right above a gorge with a blue river
still holding the cord
but it is not a cord anymore

it is the tightrope
you are on

Piranesi's Dungeons

A few legendary dreams have
taken place in Piranesi's dungeons
but everybody constantly
dreams about the walls in Piranesi's dungeons
and what is beyond

A few people have gotten lost
in their dreams in Piranesi's dungeons

but everybody constantly tries to
dream up a way to get in there

to have a look around and see
if people are suffering the way it seems

from the outside. Real suffering.
Breathless suffering, hunger and iron

But nobody is ever totally outside. We are always
inside somewhere with Piranesi watching

Pluto

Dreaming about Pluto contains a warning
albeit a friendly one
about what could happen
if you don't become nicer to other people,
even just a little bit would help

Pluto signifies
transformation, judgement, plutonium

It signifies an entity
in the shape of a planet

with a giant moon suspended from it
by the benevolent will of gravity

but the entity got lost
in outer space

and now nobody knows
where to look for it

Questions, Thirteen

Deep in the darkest hour of a very heavy week
Three earthmen did confront me, and I could hardly speak
They showed me nineteen terrors, and each one struck my soul
They threw me thirteen questions, each one an endless hole

(Kullberg & Roberts)

Thirteen questions were put to you, and you could answer none
they went on to the next even while you were still thinking
about your answer. You knew there were
going to be thirteen because it was a part of the dream
and while thinking about how far they had come
in the order of the thirteen questions
you knew you'd forgotten how many there had already been

And you learned about the magic of the number thirteen
that while you do remember how far you have come in a cycle of twelve
and in the pyramids of nine triangles

or climbing the mighty tree of seven branches, or ten
or even sixteen with plenty of steppingstones
with thirteen you are bound to always lose touch

one of them will have fallen off on the way, and while you look back
to see if it was the one between five and seven
or one of the others you just can't remember the name for right now

you realize they have begun over again. Thirteen questions,
and you can't remember the answer to a single one. That was the
weirdest dream

Quietude

In dreams, quietude comes in three forms: Noticing
the quiet in dreams is a blessing
bestowed on only a few

Not noticing the quiet in dreams
can be a mistake bigger than life

Noticing the quiet in dreams
but reacting with the purest panic known to man

will cause the cosmic landscape to change
and crumble the planets in the solar system
where even the wind has no sound

Rain

Rain. Dreaming about rain in Jerusalem
is different from dreaming about rain in New York is
very different from dreaming about
rain in the movies is very different from dreaming
about rain in the forest is not so different
from dreaming about rain in the morning you were born

Red

Dreaming about red; dreaming about red sorghum
red rosaries, reddening faces, red blood

dreaming about the red spot in the painting
dreaming about the red sunset

bursting through

dreaming about red bodies, red lies, red cars.
Humanity has a goal to live up to

and it cannot be fulfilled if you don't conquer red.
This is what the sages say. And Freud

Robot, Talking a Walk With a

The feeling of cold metal
in your hands
trying to assess

trying to assess
if the robot has fingers
so that you can hold its hands

or whether it is in fact
the robot taking you places
you don't want to go

or if you should be
anxious you haven't yet discovered
where it fastened the leash

Robot, Trying to Turn Off a

This dream has an issue of hot or cold. Any issues in
dreams are important. Nobody ever thought about
the surface temperature
of a robot before they in a dream met one
having gone AWOL or at least being really annoying
and machinelike, not at all a kind robot, and
in trying to turn it off, before you can begin to look for the switch,
you must try to find a way to determine if it is in fact
so warm you might cripple your hand or so cold your fingers will
be stuck

Rose

The Dream Weaver says:
Always fear the black rose
and don't trust the yellow
be wary, be alert for the red rose

and don't wish for the white
don't take the blue rose
as a way to heavenly spheres
even if it waves at you

to trust the purple rose
you must demand
it knows your name
and is prepared to say it

Running

Running in your dream
almost never
take you anywhere

Running in the dream
feels senseless
carrying the anxiety

in the movement itself
never in the place
you are leaving

the force you aim to avoid
dwelling inside
being the motor of running

Sex

Dreams about sex
are never as pleasant
as they say

There was always something
colliding between

your body and common ethics
don't believe Freud

believe yourself

Scorpion

scorpion, (order Scorpiones or Scorpionida),
any of approximately 1,500 elongated arachnid species
characterized by a segmented curved tail
tipped with a venomous stinger
at the rear of the body
and a pair of grasping pincers at the front
and a mastering of the force of evil
that instills much admiration
with humanoids
themselves relentlessly practicing
the sneaking upon
unexpecting fellow humanoids looking
for whatever is currently valued in the specific species

peace or money or love or laundry
or sugar or a break

Somebody Behind You

Dreaming about somebody coming up behind you
is revealing in many levels

If you hear a whispering
we are in the realm of the conscious/subconscious

If there is a tap on the shoulder
you won't lack friends in the near future

If there is a shadow creeping up on you
the somebody behind in all likelihood is yourself

Tower

Dreaming of a tower might imply any or all of these
anxiously overshadowing entities and/or existential conditions:

Identity crisis, blasphemy, fascism in your heart
The Tower of Babel, a falling body
your family forgotten and/or have forgotten you

all you ever wanted but hope, all you ever needed but rain
all you ever thought of but twilight setting in

the yearning for the sensation of holding somebody's hand

Twin, Your Lost

There was a face inside
that reminded you
of what someone once called

your true name
known only
to you and to God

who will reveal it
in due course
until then this dance with

an invisible partner

Umbrella

Dreaming about an umbrella
certainly is no sign
of comfort
or a trustworthy piece of information

who knows what you are trying
to screen yourself from,
coming from above

and who on earth knows
what above means in that context

Dreaming about two umbrellas is worse. If you have
two umbrellas you are certain
to be alone. And if you happen to be climbing

you're even worse off. And then the rain
sets in

Vacuum Cleaner

In dreams dust disappears by itself and grows by itself
just like outside of the dream. In the dream
you just never have access to a

vacuum cleaner

when you need it. Outside you don't want to use it
and/or explain to yourself you haven't got time. In dreams
all you want to do is vacuum, but there is no vacuum cleaner

In dreams the vacuum cleaner teaches us about the enigma of life
and the enigma of emotion and the short reach of free will in view

of the forces at play in a world of time and dust

Vagina

This is no dream. Morning has broken
there is a planet, there is orb

People exist. A voice is proof of breath

Last summer, last summer and orange,
the color. The sculpture. We were away

desert sun. Not anymore. Ingenious rhythm.
Resourceful time and timing. Cloud

Van Gogh (Being or Meeting Up with)

Later on, in the back alley
you're on your own
except you realize you are waiting for van Gogh
to show up

How did I get here, you wonder
you are prone to avoiding
back alleys
both day and night
but now you're on your own

you are on your own
for real except you know you are now the impersonator

he will never show

Whispering

In dreams the sound of someone whispering
is a romantic omen

In dreams the sudden sense of a whispering is a testimony
about all the lies that were told

In dreams the breath on a winter night
form a secret whispering

a soul you have yet to discover
like a beacon of unity, and hope

The Letter X

Dreaming of the letter x
is never pleasant, never fun,
never tempting, never new,

never open-minded

things lying over other things
and not in an orderly manner
fill the universe for good

Xanadu

Xanadu does in fact exist,
the mythical place of bliss. In dreams you know
where it is

and your effort to note the exact route
you took

overseas, above mountains
deep in tunnels of courage and willpower

always fails, creating a hollow recluse
you try to find a name for

Xanthippe, Being Married to

Socrates thought highly of her (more or less). In dreams,
if you are married to Xanthippe, be aware that you shall taste
as bitter drink before long. How bitter can a taste get
in a dream? It can get very, very bitter

Young Girl Crying

There was a dream once. We shall not guess as to its
content and scenery

This specific dream has been deleted
from the realm of dreams

It doesn't exist. Loose dreams
with clippings of the said nature have been

shredded in the paper mill
blown like ashes over the ocean
decomposed, dwelling in the eternal cycle of humus

If you think you've met it in a dream of a certain nature
look in the mirror. Closely. Who are you? Who are you now?

Zebra

Dreaming of stripes like that never was a very healthy sign
as it involves
more choices than is good for us

Zebras never have to choose
when they find themselves wound up in stripes
it comes naturally

they in fact are made of stripes
the same way Jaspers said to Sartre

that you don't have a body, you are a body
zebras know there are no two alike, we don't

Zenith

In dreams zenith
is an entity that moves
at the same speed

as it is approached
by the subject
aiming to eliminate it

by a shameless presence
overshadowing
its absolute nature

All dreams aim for
the absolute
Not all dreamers do

Zero

In many parts of the world
zero doesn't even exist,
in the sphere of emotion, it is not recognized
in the world of guilt
it is much revered but very seldom, if ever,
attained

in the realm of intention
it is a common enough joke
albeit dialectic

in mathematics it is sincerely doubted
by researchers of merit

in chronology
it is out of the question
since everything begins after it is gone

so, how can you dream of it? It's
easy. There is always a hole somewhere
in the dreamscape of desire

Zorro

These are dreams of an acute nature
dreaming in black and white is most appropriate
but more often it is the colored version
of the films from your daddy's childhood

where Zorro's hair is grey
and his horse's tail too

which is something you discovered
just before you wake up

wondering who actually
cut the bloody z

right across your chest
and when it happened

since you did not feel the sting
as the melancholy flood

you spent your night in was soothing
on a whole other level

Books by Jakob Brønnum

A little book of transcendence (2023)

The Road to Tremonte (2024)

The Poetry Encyclopedia of Dreams (2025)

Dreamscape Journeys (2025)

www.ingramcontent.com/pod-product-compliance
Lightning Source LLC
LaVergne TN
LVHW051453170726
843492LV00002B/667